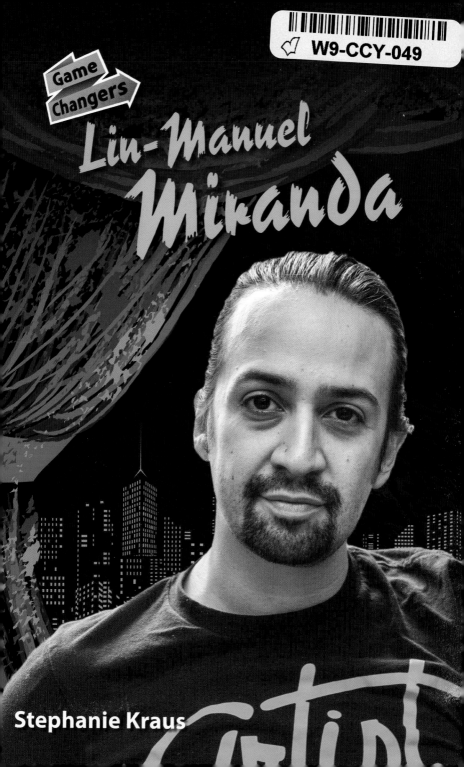

Game Changers

Lin-Manuel Miranda

Stephanie Kraus

Consultants

Timothy Rasinski, Ph.D.
Kent State University

Lori Oczkus, M.A.
Literacy Consultant

Publishing Credits

Rachelle Cracchiolo, M.S.Ed., *Publisher*

Conni Medina, M.A.Ed., *Managing Editor*

Dona Herweck Rice, *Series Developer*

Emily R. Smith, M.A.Ed., *Content Director*

Seth Rogers/Noelle Cristea, M.A.Ed., *Editors*

Robin Erickson, *Senior Graphic Designer*

The TIME logo is a registered trademark of TIME Inc. Used under license.

Image Credits: Cover and p.1 (front) John D. & Catherine T. MacArthur Foundation, (back) Theo Wargo/WireImage/Getty Images; Reader's Guide page William Thomas Cain/Getty Images; p.2 Shahar Azran/WireImage/Getty Images; p.4 (left) REUTERSAlamy Stock Photo, (right) Courtesy of Lin-Manuel Miranda; p.5 United States Government/Public Domain; p.6 Courtesy of Lin-Manuel Miranda; p.7 (left) The Advertising ArchivesAlamy Stock Photo, (center) Black StarAlamy Stock Photo, (right) moviesAlamy Stock Photo; p.9 Courtesy of Lin-Manuel Miranda; pp.10–11 Joe Mabel; p.11 Bruce Glikas/FilmMagic/Getty Images; p.13 Brent N. Clarke/Getty Images; p.14 Everett Collection Inc/Alamy Stock Photo; p.18 Walter McBride/Getty Images; p.19 Neilson Barnard/Getty Images; p.21 Walter McBride/Getty Images; pp.24–25 REUTERS/Alamy Stock Photo; p.26 Walter McBride/WireImage/Getty Images; p.29 and back page The Pulitzer Prizes/Columbia University; all other images from iStock and/or Shutterstock.

Teacher Created Materials

5301 Oceanus Drive
Huntington Beach, CA 92649-1030
http://www.tcmpub.com

ISBN 978-1-4938-3930-8

© 2017 Teacher Created Materials, Inc.
Printed in China
Nordica.072018.CA21800845

Table of Contents

Rewriting History

Lin-Manuel Miranda was casually looking around a bookstore one day when he came across *Alexander Hamilton* by Ron Chernow. He bought the bestselling biography and began reading it on vacation in Mexico. After a few chapters, Miranda was hooked. The book describes how Hamilton, an orphan from the Caribbean, wrote his way out of poverty and overcame all odds to help shape a new nation. Miranda was inspired. He wanted to bring the Founding Father's journey to life in a new way. He started rewriting the story—this time as a rap and hip-hop musical.

Presidential Praise

First Lady Michelle Obama called *Hamilton* "the best piece of art in any form that I have ever seen in my life." President Barack Obama said, "The first thing we thought about was what could we do to encourage this kind of creativity in teaching history to our kids."

The Room Where It Happened

In 2009, just one year after Miranda's vacation, the White House held its first ever Evening of Poetry, Music, and the Spoken Word. Miranda was invited to perform. He thought it was the perfect time to try out one of his songs from *The Hamilton Mixtape,* which he would later rename *Hamilton: An American Musical.* "[It's] about the life of somebody who **embodies** hip-hop, Treasury Secretary Alexander Hamilton," Miranda joked with the room.

The crowd laughed at the idea, but by the end of the song, they were giving him a standing ovation. Now, *Hamilton* is one of the most successful musicals of all time. And Miranda is the creative genius behind it.

Raised on Hip-Hop and Broadway

Miranda was born on January 16, 1980, in New York City. He was raised in Inwood, a mostly Hispanic neighborhood on the northern tip of Manhattan. His mother, Luz Towns-Miranda, was a clinical psychologist. His father, Luis A. Miranda Jr., worked in politics. He served as an advisor to New York City Mayor Ed Koch and became well known in the Latino community. His parents, both born in Puerto Rico, often returned to the island with Lin-Manuel during the summer months.

A Young Ham

Miranda started taking piano lessons when he was six. At his first recital, Miranda heard the applause and wanted to stay on the stage. "After the fourth round, the teacher gently pushed him off the piano so other kids could play," Luis Miranda told the *New York Times*.

Luis Miranda loved musical theater, but the family didn't have the money to see many shows. However, a young Lin-Manuel was able to see *Les Misérables*, *Cats*, and *The Phantom of the Opera*—or, as he calls them, "the holy trinity." He says his family home was filled with show tunes and salsa music. Miranda's school bus driver happened to love rap. His daily bus rides were one place where Miranda learned many rap lyrics growing up.

Playing to His Strengths

Miranda attended Hunter College Elementary School in New York City. He spoke English at school, but he spoke Spanish with his family at home. "It's a great way of creating a writer because you're aware of being an outsider," he says. "You change identities when you go home and any time you can try a different identity that's helpful in being a writer or performer."

Miranda went on to attend Hunter College High School, a school for intellectually gifted students. Miranda says he never felt like the smartest person in the room, so he worked hard to find his **niche**—which he found in musical theater. He became very involved in his school's drama department. In ninth grade, he played one of the lead roles in *The Pirates of Penzance* by Gilbert and Sullivan. During that show, he was able to meet Broadway legend Stephen Sondheim, who later became a mentor to him.

Sondheim

Composer and **lyricist** Stephen Sondheim has worked in musical theater for over 50 years. His works include *Into the Woods*, *Sweeney Todd*, and the lyrics in *West Side Story*. In 2008, he worked with Miranda to translate *West Side Story* into Spanish. In return, Sondheim later gave Miranda notes on *Hamilton*.

Lovestruck

In sixth grade, Miranda was cast as Conrad Birdie in *Bye Bye Birdie*. "It's the best part when you're 12 years old because every girl in the grade pretends to be in love with you," he says.

Climbing to New Heights

After high school, Miranda studied theater and film at Wesleyan University in Connecticut. As a sophomore, he began writing his first musical, *In the Heights*. The story centers on a **bodega** in the Washington Heights neighborhood in New York City. Miranda was the show's creator and composer.

Miranda graduated from college in 2002 and started acting in television and film. He worked part-time jobs so he could devote time to writing. He was a substitute teacher at his former high school, reviewed restaurants, and wrote jingles for commercials.

Freestylin'

While in college, Miranda cofounded a comedy **improv** group called Freestyle Love Supreme. Five performers turn ideas from the audience into hip-hop shows, right on the spot. The group still performs regularly in New York City and across the country.

Early Success

Throughout his twenties, Miranda continued working on *In the Heights*. He partnered with Wesleyan graduate and friend Thomas Kail, who went on to direct the play. The show, with Miranda as the lead, made its Broadway debut in 2008 and was an instant success. For the first time, audiences could hear Miranda's ability to beautifully blend the diverse music of his childhood.

In 2008, *In the Heights* was nominated for 13 Tony Awards®. The show won four, including Best Musical. Miranda rhymed his acceptance speech for Best Original Score. The show was also nominated for the 2009 Pulitzer Prize for Drama—**foreshadowing** what was to come.

The Never-Ending Résumé

Miranda was the co-composer and co-lyricist of Broadway's *Bring It On: The Musical*, which was **nominated** for two Tony Awards—Best Musical and Best Choreography.

Hamilton in the Making

It took Miranda six years to write *Hamilton*. His White House performance helped open some doors. He turned his idea into a stage musical at the downtown Public Theater in New York City. Miranda wanted to work with his *In the Heights* team again. He asked Thomas Kail to be the director, Alex Lacamoire to be the music director, and Andy Blankenbuehler to be the choreographer. The team also worked with Oskar Eustis, the artistic director for Public Theater.

Ron Chernow was a natural choice to act as the show's historical advisor since his book had inspired Miranda. Together, they made sure that the show was as historically accurate as possible. However, Miranda did take artistic liberties by exaggerating some story lines and relationships. Their work earned them an award from the New-York Historical Society.

#ham4ham

In the first year of its Broadway release, *Hamilton* was almost always sold out, but people could enter a lottery two hours before the show to try to win unclaimed seats. So many people showed up that Miranda started #ham4ham performances two days a week to entertain fans waiting outside the theater.

Ron Chernow

Andy Blankenbuehler

The more Miranda learned about Alexander Hamilton, the more parallels he saw between the hip-hop world and Hamilton's life. Hamilton was a poor orphan with a difficult childhood. But, he had a way with words and earned himself a scholarship for his writing. Miranda saw similar stories reflected in the lives of other hip-hop artists.

The Creative Process

Miranda has been called a creative genius, but what exactly is his creative process? He writes mostly in motion—brainstorming melodies on walks near his home and humming lyrics on the subway. When a song starts to crystallize, he records a rough version on his laptop or phone.

Lin-Manuel Miranda

Oskar Eustis

Thomas Kail

Alex Lacamoire

A Diverse Cast

From the start, Miranda envisioned a racially mixed cast for the show. He cast African American, Hispanic, Asian, and Latino actors to play the historical figures, who were all white. Many theatergoers applauded the move. But some believed it did not paint an accurate portrait of the country's history.

In 2016, the press criticized one of *Hamilton*'s open casting calls that specifically asked for people of color. The Actors' Equity Association theater union said that denying white performers the chance to audition was wrong. The show changed the language of its casting call to make it clear that everyone was welcome to audition, but Miranda's vision for the cast didn't change. "The reality is, we've always had white ensemble members. That's always been a part of the show."

original cast of *Hamilton*

Miranda defends an author's right to cast a s[...]
however he or she sees fit. He says that the castin[...]
a bridge for the audience. "The reason *Hamilton*[...]
is because there is no distance between that story[...]
happened 200-some-odd years ago and now," Mi[...]
Latina magazine, "because it looks like America[...]

Inspired By . . .

Hispanic performers
have always inspired
Miranda. Two of his
role models are Rubén
Blades and Rita Moreno.

Latino 3%

Asian
American 9%

African
American
17%

STOP!
THIN[K]

This chart from the [...]
American Performer[...]
Coalition represents[...]
percentages for acto[...]
color on New York st[...]

◎ How do you thin[...]
chart might cha[...]
the next 10 year[...]

◎ What conclusion[...]
drawn from this[...]

Diversity by Numbers

Lin-Manuel Miranda has made it a point to focus on **diversity** in *Hamilton*. He has not only used different genres of music but also chosen to cast a significantly diverse group of people to depict the all-white historical figures. Compare New York City theater statistics to the population of New York City in order to understand why the diversity in *Hamilton*'s cast has been viewed as a groundbreaking part of Broadway history.

Broadway Audiences (2014–15)

66% of audience members were female.

44 was the average age of Broadway audience members.

88% of all tickets were purchased by Caucasians.

Casting Breakdown by Ethnicity in NYC Theaters, Nine-Year Combined Average (2006–15)

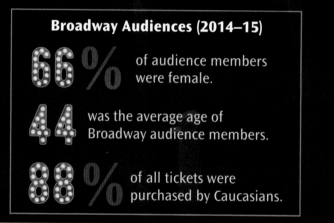

4% Asian

3% Latino

less than 1% all other minorities

15% African American

78% Caucasian

Numbers may total more than 100% due to rounding.

Source: AAPAC

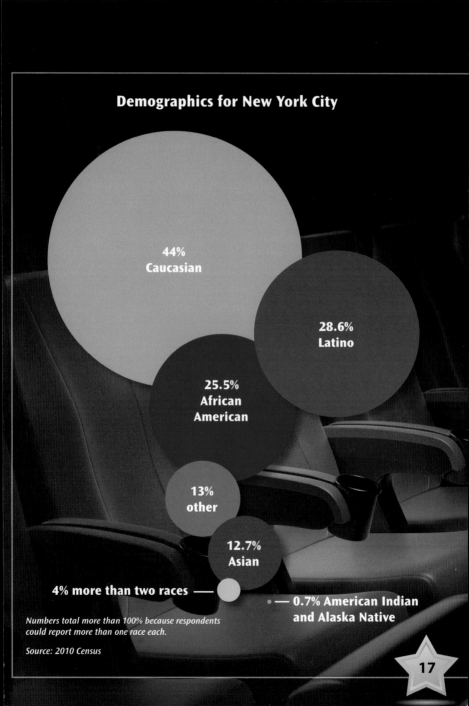

Demographics for New York City

44%
Caucasian

28.6%
Latino

25.5%
African
American

13%
other

12.7%
Asian

4% more than two races ——

—— 0.7% American Indian
and Alaska Native

*Numbers total more than 100% because respondents
could report more than one race each.*

Source: 2010 Census

17

Best of Women

Along with his commitment to diversity, Miranda made sure women shared the stage in his shows. Hamilton's wife, Elizabeth (Eliza), and her sisters were an important part of his journey. "The show reminds us that this nation was built by more than just a few great men," President Obama says.

Actress Renée Goldsberry played Angelica Schuyler, Hamilton's sister-in-law, in the original cast. "We have the opportunity to reclaim a history that some of us don't necessarily think is our own," she told *TIME* magazine.

Miranda spoke about the casting of women at the Smithsonian Museum of American History when he said, "I'm totally open to women playing Founding Fathers once this goes into the world."

Jasmine Cephas Jones

Phillipa Soo

Renée Goldsberry

Best of Wives

Miranda credits much of his own success to the woman by his side, his wife, Vanessa Adriana Nadal. The two met in high school, but they didn't reconnect until years after college. He saw that she liked hip-hop and salsa on a social media profile and invited Nadal to his freestyle show. The two got married in 2010.

Nadal is a scientist who now works as an attorney. She encourages Miranda to take time for writing. "He's very **empathetic** and good at putting himself in other people's shoes, and I think that's why he can write women in a way that other men can't," she told Fordham News.

On November 10, 2014, the couple welcomed their first child, Sebastian. He was born just two weeks before *Hamilton*'s Off-Broadway rehearsals began. "She's the superhero in all of this because she had to deal with a newborn kid during **tech** [rehearsals]," Miranda told Playbill.com.

Disney Dreams

Miranda worked on the music for Disney•Pixar's animated movie, *Moana*. The directors for *Moana* also directed *The Little Mermaid*, which is Miranda's favorite movie of all time. He says sharing *Moana* as his son's first movie is ". . . a dream come true for me."

Giving Back

In 2015, Miranda won a MacArthur Foundation Fellowship for *Hamilton*. The award is known as the "genius grant." Winners can use the $625,000 prize however they want, no questions asked. Miranda chose to use it on **charities**. Part of it went to Graham Windham, a nonprofit started by Elizabeth Hamilton in 1806. This agency helps low-income children and families. Some of the money went to the Mariposa Center, a group that helps girls in the Dominican Republic with a wide range of services.

The producers of *Hamilton* also teamed up with the Rockefeller Foundation. Together, they created the Hamilton Education Program. It gives 20,000 New York City public high school students the chance to see the show that is often sold out. Students are charged $10— the bill with Hamilton's face on it. Many students now study the show and the history behind it.

Show and Tell

The Hamilton Education Program included an interactive program for classrooms. The students presented creative and artistic historical research projects and shared them with the show's cast. Miranda often tweeted his excitement about seeing their projects.

THINK LINK

- How does *Hamilton* connect to classrooms?

- Why might Miranda want to offer discounted tickets to students?

- If you were asked to create your own artistic, historical research project, what topic would you choose? How would you present it?

Helping Puerto Rico

Because his father was a politician, Miranda says he has an aversion to politics. But he felt compelled to help the U.S. territory of Puerto Rico. On March 15, 2016, Miranda called on Congress to help solve Puerto Rico's economic crisis. The island faced a $72 billion **debt** for its 3.5 million residents. Families were forced to **emigrate** as schools and hospitals closed.

Miranda pointed out that if Puerto Rico were a U.S. city, instead of a territory, it would get more help. "If a ship is sinking, you don't ask, 'Well, what type of ship is it and what type of ship should it be?' You rescue the people aboard."

Miracles Happen

Miranda talked about his heritage when he was asked to speak at the 2016 University of Pennsylvania commencement. He cited the negative **rhetoric** used for **immigrants** during the 2016 presidential election. He reminded the crowd that Hamilton was a poor immigrant. "Time and time again, immigrants get the job done." He encouraged the graduates to share their stories. "I know that many of you made miracles happen to get to this day," Miranda said. ". . . I know because my family made miracles happen for me to be standing here, talking to you, telling stories."

Summers in Puerto Rico

Miranda said he learned to love Puerto Rico by spending summers there as a kid. He sold snacks to students going back to school in August.

Building a Legacy

In 2016, *Hamilton* was nominated for 16 Tony Awards and won 11 trophies. The show won Best Musical, and Miranda took home trophies for Best Score and Best Book of a Musical. Tragically, on the morning of the awards event, a gunman shot and killed 49 innocent people in Orlando, Florida. When Miranda took the stage, he read a sonnet about love and acceptance. "Love is love is love is love is love is love is love is love," Miranda told the crowd. "Now fill the world with music, love, and pride."

Final Bow

After almost a year playing the lead role, Miranda stepped down on July 9, 2016. His alternate, Javier Muñoz, was ready to step in. He was Miranda's alternate during *In the Heights* and was already playing Hamilton when Miranda was not scheduled to perform. The original cast filmed two performances before taking their final bows together. "I think this is a role I'm going to be going back to again and again," Miranda reassured reporters.

Pulitzer!

Hamilton won the Pulitzer Prize for Drama in April 2016. It was the ninth musical to win the prestigious honor since the award began in 1916. Other winners include *Rent* and *A Chorus Line*.

MacPEGOT

All of these awards mean that Miranda only needs to win an Oscar to be the first person with a "MacPEGOT." This could be the nickname for someone who wins each of the following awards: MacArthur Foundation Fellowship, Pulitzer Prize, Emmy, Grammy, Oscar, and Tony.

Who Tells Our Story?

The final number in *Hamilton*, "Who Lives, Who Dies, Who Tells Your Story," is sung by Eliza. After her husband dies in a duel at age 49, Eliza Hamilton lives for another 50 years—dedicating her time to continuing his work and protecting his **legacy**. Miranda says the show invites the audience to think about the legacy we leave behind. "When we're faced with what Hamilton got done in his life, it feels like three lifetimes' worth," he told *TIME*. "Everyone who leaves the theater goes 'Wow. Well, what am I doing with my life? What is my legacy?'"

Miranda's legacy has already made a lasting mark on musical theater. He has challenged how stories are told and who has the right to tell them. "What I hope is the positive legacy of this show is that you have a cast full of incredible actors of color—there's no movie stars in it—and it's doing well," he told *TIME*. "That gives me hope that future productions realize having a cast that reflects what our country looks like eliminates distance between the contemporary audience and this story that happened over 200 years ago." What's next for Miranda's legacy is unknown, but with any luck, audiences are only witnessing the first act of his career.

Advice for Young Artists

Miranda says, "Focus on the thing you're not good at. If you're a good singer, go take dance lessons. If you're a good dancer, take singing lessons. This way when you go for an audition, they say, 'This person can do everything.' You want to be that undeniable person."

Glossary

bodega—a small grocery store found in urban areas

charities—organizations that help those in need

composer—a person who writes music, especially as a professional occupation

debt—something, typically money, that is owed or due

diversity—the state of having people who are different races or who have different cultures in a group or organization

embodies—represents an idea, quality, or feeling

emigrate—to leave one's country to live somewhere else

empathetic—able to understand and share the feelings of another

foreshadowing—warning or indication (a future event)

immigrants—people who settle in a country to live

improv—short for improvisation, the art of performing without previous preparation

legacy—the way one is remembered

lyricist—a person who writes the words to a song or musical

niche—a place, employment, status, or activity for which a person or thing is best fitted

nominated—proposed or formally entered as a candidate for election, honor, or award

rhetoric—language intended to influence people

tech (technical rehearsal)—a rehearsal, usually held shortly before opening night, at which sound, lighting, and other technical operations are practiced

Index

Check It Out!

Books

Alegria Hudes, Quiara, and Lin-Manuel Miranda. 2013.
*In the Heights: The Complete Book and Lyrics of
the Broadway Musical (Applause Libretto Library).*
Applause Theatre & Cinema Books.

Chernow, Ron. 2005. *Alexander Hamilton*. Penguin Books.

Fritz, Jean. 2012. *Alexander Hamilton: The Outsider*.
Puffin Books.

Miranda, Lin-Manuel, and Jeremy McCarter. 2016.
Hamilton: The Revolution. Grand Central Publishing.

Video

The White House. "Rose Garden Freestyle feat.
Lin-Manuel Miranda."

Websites

Lin-Manuel Miranda and 5000 Broadway Productions.
Lin-Manuel Miranda. http://www.linmanuel.com/.

The New York Times. "Lin-Manuel Miranda: By the
Book." http://www.nytimes.com/2016/04/10/books/
review/lin-manuel-miranda-by-the-book.html.

TIME FOR KIDS. An Interview with Lin-Manuel Miranda.
http://www.timeforkids.com/news/interview-lin-manuel
-miranda/270366.

TIME Magazine. TIME 100 Pioneers: Lin-Manuel Miranda
by J. J. Abrams. http://time.com/4299633/lin-manuel
-miranda-2016-time-100/.

Try It!

Act 2 of *Hamilton* focuses on the foundational differences between Alexander Hamilton's beliefs and Thomas Jefferson's beliefs. Miranda uses rap battles to depict the differences between the Hamiltonians (Federalists) and the Jeffersonians (Democratic-Republicans). Imagine you are tasked with writing a rap battle about a core difference between the two political parties. To get started, you have some research to do:

◎ Research the Federalist Party and the Democratic-Republican Party.

◎ List opposing viewpoints about banking, the economy, the power of the states, and who was allowed to vote.

◎ Select one of these issues to research.

◎ Here's where you will need to select a side to align with. Do you agree more with the Federalists or the Democratic-Republicans regarding the issue? You'll need to know in depth how your side felt about the issue.

◎ Prepare a rap battle in which the Federalist Party and the Democratic-Republican Party go back and forth on your selected issue. Make sure that even though both sides are represented in the battle, your side is the clear winner at the end.

About the Author

Stephanie Kraus was born in Brooklyn, New York, and raised in Hazlet, New Jersey. She performed in musicals in high school, but none *quite* as good as *Hamilton*. She studied communication and journalism at the University of Delaware and is currently a producer for *TIME FOR KIDS* magazine in New York City. In her free time, she enjoys seeing Broadway shows with her boyfriend, Anthony. She is looking forward to taking her niece, Faith, to see Disney's *Moana* and Miranda's next big hit.